THE LIFE OF

MALALA YOUSAFZAI

BY ELIZABETH RAUM

AMICUS | AMICUS INK

Sequence is published by Amicus and Amicus Ink
P.O. Box 1329, Mankato, MN 56002
www.amicuspublishing.us

Library of Congress Cataloging-in-Publication Data
Names: Raum, Elizabeth, author.
Title: The life of Malala Yousafzai / by Elizabeth Raum.
Description: Mankato, Minnesota : Amicus, [2020] | Series: Sequence. Change Maker Biographies | Audience: Grades: K to Grade 3. | Includes webography. | Includes index.
Identifiers: LCCN 2018030066 (print) | LCCN 2018033591 (ebook) | ISBN 9781681517599 (pdf) | ISBN 9781681516776 (Library Binding) | ISBN 9781681524634 (Paperback)
Subjects: LCSH: Yousafzai, Malala, 1997---Juvenile literature. | Sex discrimination in education--Pakistan. | Girls--Education--Pakistan--Juvenile literature. | Women social reformers--Pakistan--Biography--Juvenile literature. | Political activists--Pakistan--Biography.
Classification: LCC LC2330 (ebook) | LCC LC2330 .R38 2020 (print) | DDC 371.822095491--dc23
LC record available at https://lccn.loc.gov/2018030066

Editor: Alissa Thielges
Designer: Ciara Beitlich
Photo Researcher: Holly Young

Photo Credits: Getty/Richard Stonehouse / Stringer cover; Shutterstock/khlongwangchao cover, 17; Wiki/Attribution 3.0 Unported (CC BY 3.0) 4–5; Wiki/Attribution-ShareAlike 3.0 Unported (CC BY-SA 3.0) 6–7; Newscom/slb pak Xinhua News Agency 9; AP/John Stillwell / EMPPL PA Wire 10–11; Getty/Veronique de Viguerie 10, 13; Getty/A MAJEED / Stringer 14; YouTube/Class Dismissed in Swat Valley - Malala Yousafzai News | The New York Times 14; Newscom/Pakistan Press International Photo 18–19; Newscom/Max Becherer/Polaris 21; Getty/Queen Elizabeth Hospital Birmingham 22–23; Newscom/Dennis Van Tine/ABACAUSA.COM 25; Newscom/Poppe, Cornelius/ZUMA Press 26; Getty/ABDUL MAJEED / AFP 28–29

Printed in the United States of America

HC 10 9 8 7 6 5 4 3 2 1
PB 10 9 8 7 6 5 4 3 2 1

TABLE OF CONTENTS

Who is Malala Yousafzai?

Malala Yousafzai [muh-LAH-luh YOO-suhf-zigh] was ten years old when the Taliban, a terrorist group, invaded her city, Mingora, Pakistan. They closed her school and many others. She began to speak out against this. She believes that every child deserves an education. She says, "One child, one teacher, one book, and one pen can change the world."

Malala is an **activist** for children's education.

LOADING . . LOADING . . LOADING . . .

Mingora is between two mountain ranges.

Malala is born.

LOADING . . . LOADING . .

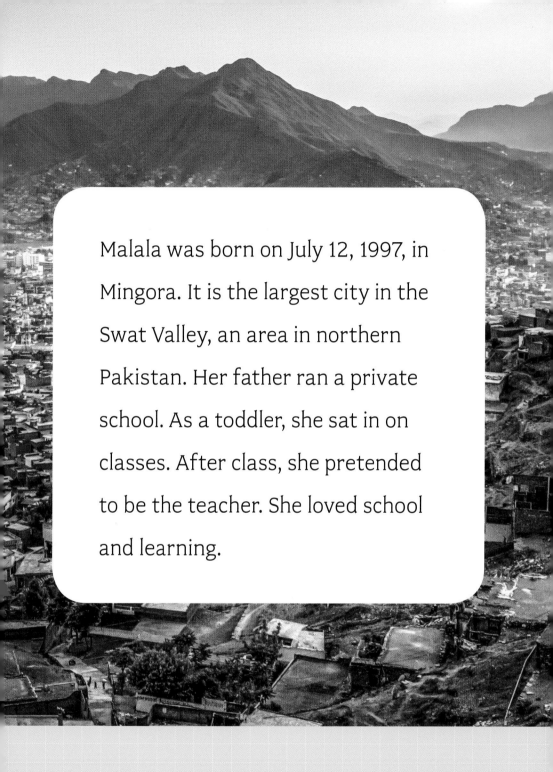

Malala was born on July 12, 1997, in Mingora. It is the largest city in the Swat Valley, an area in northern Pakistan. Her father ran a private school. As a toddler, she sat in on classes. After class, she pretended to be the teacher. She loved school and learning.

Living in Fear

In 2007, the Taliban took over the Swat Valley. They are a terrorist group. Malala was 10. People were forced to obey strict **Islamic** laws. Anyone who spoke out against the Taliban was attacked. By 2008, they had bombed 200 schools and closed over 400.

A school in Pakistan is in ruins after Taliban bombings.

Malala is born.

JULY 12, 1997   2008   DING . . . LOADING .

Taliban closes 400 schools.

Malala is born.

Malala gives first speech.

JULY 12, 1997   2008   SEPT. 1, 2008   ...LOADING.

Taliban closes 400 schools.

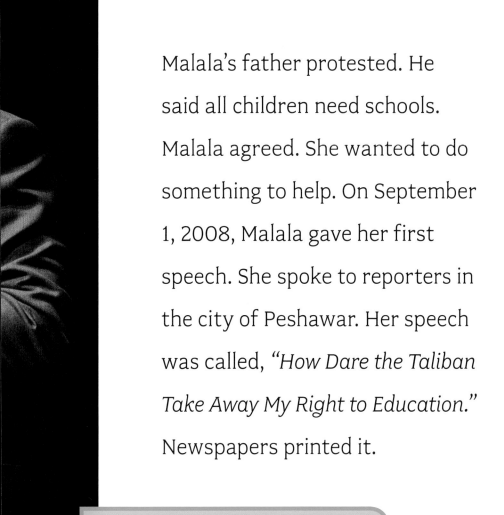

Malala's father protested. He said all children need schools. Malala agreed. She wanted to do something to help. On September 1, 2008, Malala gave her first speech. She spoke to reporters in the city of Peshawar. Her speech was called, *"How Dare the Taliban Take Away My Right to Education."* Newspapers printed it.

Malala's father speaks out against the Taliban.

LOADING . . . LOADING . . . LOADING . . .

Fighting Back

A reporter for the **BBC** spoke with Malala's dad. The BBC wanted a girl to write about daily life under the Taliban. Malala said, "Why not me?" She began on January 3, 2009. Her first story was called "I Am Afraid." She wrote 35 stories using a fake name. She told no one.

Malala is born.

Malala gives first speech.

JULY 12, 1997   2008   SEPT. 1, 2008   JAN. 2009

Taliban closes 400 schools.

Malala writes her first story for the BBC.

Malala wrote under the name Gul Makai. It is a name from a folk tale.

LOADING.. LOADING.. LOADING...

I want to get my education, and I want to become a doctor...

Malala is born.	Malala gives first speech.	Malala stars in a documentary.

JULY 12, 1997	2008	SEPT. 1, 2008	JAN. 2009	SPRING 2009

Taliban closes 400 schools.	Malala writes her first story for the BBC.

The Taliban grew stronger. They ordered 50,000 girls in the Swat Valley to stop going to school. Malala was angry and afraid. Her family fled the area for three months. When they came back, Malala agreed to be in a **documentary**. She wanted to tell her story. She thought it would help others.

Malala and her dad (top left) spoke in a documentary. Below, girls in Pakistan attend school.

Malala spoke for all children in Pakistan. She said that every girl and boy deserves a good education. By 2010, people in Pakistan knew that she had written the BBC stories. Reporters interviewed her and she gave more speeches. She said she was afraid of the Taliban. She wanted a better future for Pakistan. She wanted schools.

A class of Pakistani girls gets ready to learn.

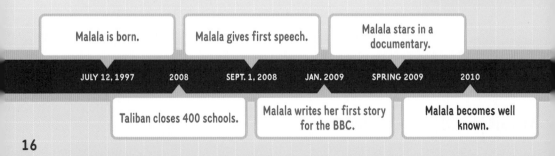

Malala is born.

Malala gives first speech.

Malala stars in a documentary.

JULY 12, 1997   2008   SEPT. 1, 2008   JAN. 2009   SPRING 2009   2010

Taliban closes 400 schools.

Malala writes her first story for the BBC.

Malala becomes well known.

Malala is born.

Malala gives first speech.

Malala stars in a documentary.

JULY 12, 1997   2008   SEPT. 1, 2008   JAN. 2009   SPRING 2009   2010

Taliban closes 400 schools.

Malala writes her first story for the BBC.

Malala becomes well known.

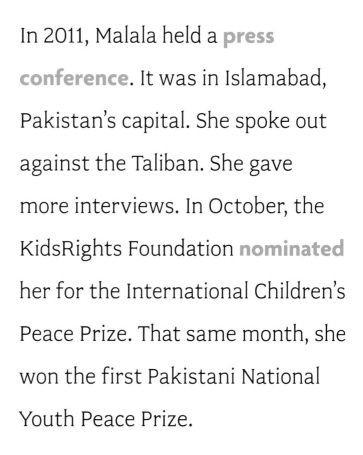

In 2011, Malala held a **press conference**. It was in Islamabad, Pakistan's capital. She spoke out against the Taliban. She gave more interviews. In October, the KidsRights Foundation **nominated** her for the International Children's Peace Prize. That same month, she won the first Pakistani National Youth Peace Prize.

Pakistan's Prime Minister presents the peace prize to Malala.

Malala wins the Pakistani National Youth Peace Prize.

2011

LOADING . . . LOADING . . .

Attacked!

Speaking out was dangerous for Malala. The Taliban fought back. On October 9, 2012, Malala was riding home from school when a man stopped the bus. A gunman jumped inside. "Which one is Malala?" he asked. No one spoke, but some looked at her. The gunman fired. The bullet hit Malala in the head.

Malala is born.

Malala gives first speech.

Malala stars in a documentary.

JULY 12, 1997　　2008　　SEPT. 1, 2008　　JAN. 2009　　SPRING 2009　　2010

Taliban closes 400 schools.

Malala writes her first story for the BBC.

Malala becomes well known.

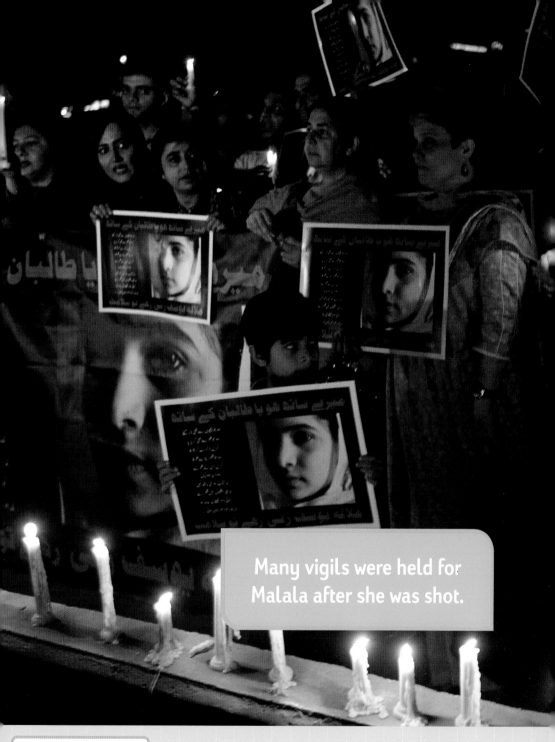

Many vigils were held for Malala after she was shot.

ING . . LOADING . . .

Malala did not die. She was rushed to the hospital. Four days later, she was flown to Birmingham, England. She had many surgeries. Slowly, she began to get better. Her story made the news. People all over the world sent her well wishes. Her family joined her in England. In March 2013, she began school there.

Malala while in the hospital, pictured here with her brothers and dad.

Malala is born.	Malala gives first speech.	Malala stars in a documentary.	
JULY 12, 1997 — 2008 — SEPT. 1, 2008 — JAN. 2009 — SPRING 2009 — 2010

| | Taliban closes 400 schools. | Malala writes her first story for the BBC. | Malala becomes well known. |

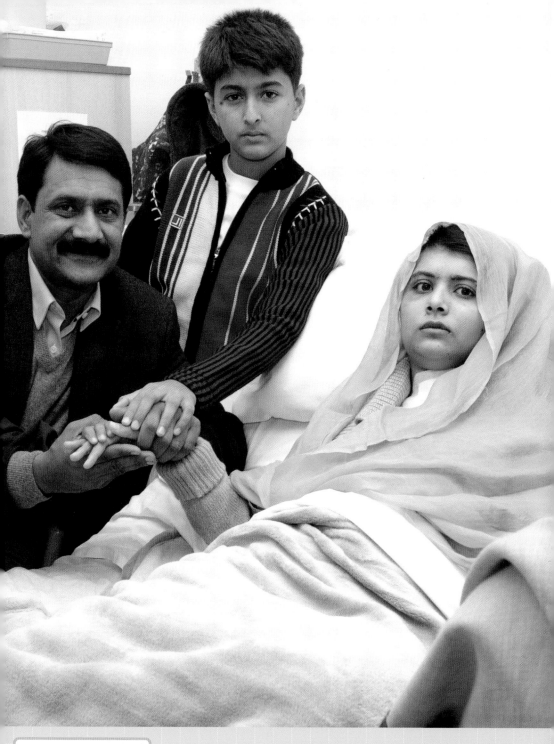

Malala wins the Pakistani National Youth Peace Prize.

Malala recovers and attends school in England.

2011   OCT. 9, 2012   MARCH 2013

...LOADING...

Malala is shot in the head.

23

Speaking to the World

On July 12, 2013, Malala spoke at the United Nations Youth Assembly in New York. It was her 16th birthday. She said, "I am here to speak for the right of education for every child." She wrote a book called *I Am Malala*. She writes, "Peace in every home, every street, every village, every country—this is my dream."

| Malala is born. | Malala gives first speech. | Malala stars in a documentary. |

| JULY 12, 1997 | 2008 | SEPT. 1, 2008 | JAN. 2009 | SPRING 2009 | 2010 |

| Taliban closes 400 schools. | Malala writes her first story for the BBC. | Malala becomes well known. |

Malala speaks to 1,000 young leaders at the youth assembly in 2013.

Malala wins the Pakistani National Youth Peace Prize.

Malala recovers and attends school in England.

2011   OCT. 9, 2012   MARCH 2013   JULY 12, 2013

Malala is shot in the head.

Malala speaks at United Nations.

Malala is born.

Malala gives first speech.

Malala stars in a documentary.

JULY 12, 1997   2008   SEPT. 1, 2008   JAN. 2009   SPRING 2009   2010

Taliban closes 400 schools.

Malala writes her first story for the BBC.

Malala becomes well known.

In 2014, she founded the Malala Fund. It supports schools for girls. She visited girls in Jordan, Kenya and Nigeria. She spoke at conferences around the world. In October 2014, she won the **Nobel Peace Prize**. It is one of the world's greatest honors. At 17, she was the youngest winner ever.

Malala is the first Pakistani to win the Nobel Peace Prize.

Malala wins the Pakistani National Youth Peace Prize.

Malala recovers and attends school in England.

Establishes Malala Fund; wins Nobel Peace Prize.

| 2011 | OCT. 9, 2012 | MARCH 2013 | JULY 12, 2013 | OCTOBER 2014 |

Malala is shot in the head.

Malala speaks at United Nations.

In October 2017, Malala began college at Oxford University in England. For now, she and her family live there. Malala visited Pakistan in 2018 under heavy guard. She prays for peace in her native land. She believes every child should have a good education. Malala plans to make her dreams come true.

Malala is born.

Malala gives first speech.

Malala stars in a documentary.

JULY 12, 1997   2008   SEPT. 1, 2008   JAN. 2009   SPRING 2009   2010

Taliban closes 400 schools.

Malala writes her first story for the BBC.

Malala becomes well known.

Malala poses for a picture on her visit to Pakistan. Mingora, her home city, is in the background.

Malala wins the Pakistani National Youth Peace Prize.		Malala recovers and attends school in England.		Establishes Malala Fund; wins Nobel Peace Prize.	
2011	OCT. 9, 2012	MARCH 2013	JULY 12, 2013	OCTOBER 2014	OCTOBER 2017
	Malala is shot in the head.		Malala speaks at United Nations.		Begins college at Oxford.

Glossary

activist Someone who works to bring about political or social change.

BBC British Broadcasting Corporation; a television and news organization that is funded by the government in the United Kingdom.

documentary A television program or movie based on real events.

Islamic Based on the religious faith of Muslims and their Holy Scriptures.

Nobel Peace Prize A prize awarded each year to a person who has done important work in encouraging peace and charity throughout the world.

nominate To suggest that someone would be the right person for an honor or award.

press conference A pre-arranged meeting with news reporters.

Taliban An Islamic group that began in Afghanistan in 1994. This group uses violence to force people to follow their strict rules.

terrorist Someone who uses violence or threats to frighten people into obeying.

Read More

Brown, Dinah. *Who is Malala Yousafzai?* New York: Grosset & Dunlap, 2015.

Frier, Raphaële. *Malala: Activist for Girls' Education.* Watertown, Mass.: Charlesbridge, 2017.

Yousafzai, Malala. *Malala's Magic Pencil.* New York: Little Brown and Company, 2017.

Websites

Kids Rights | Malala Yousafzai
https://kidsrights.org/malala-yousafzai

Malala Fund | Malala's Story
https://www.malala.org/malalas-story

The Nobel Prize | Malala Yousafsai: Facts
https://www.nobelprize.org/prizes/peace/2014/ yousafzai/facts/

Index

About the Author

Elizabeth Raum has written over 100 books for young readers. Many are biographies. She enjoys learning about people who help us see the world in new and exciting ways. She lives in Fargo, North Dakota. To learn more, visit her website: www.ElizabethRaumBooks.com.